Tough Skin

by Sylvia A. Thomas

[AP]

Unless otherwise indicated, Bible quotations are taken from the NIV version of the Bible. Copyright© 1988, 1989, 1990, 1991 by Tyndale House Publishers, Inc.

Tough Skin
By Sylvia A. Thomas

Printed in the United States of America

Published by:
[AP]
Amani Publishing
P. O. Box 12045
Tallahassee, FL 32317
850-264-3341 phone
850-878-1006 fax

A publishing company based on faith, hope, and love

Visit us at: www.AmaniPublishing.net

Email us at: AmaniPublishing@aol.com

ISBN: 0975285165

Library of Congress Number: 2006930545

Cover photo provided by: www.Istockphoto.com

Contents

Dedication

This book is lovingly dedicated to my Lord and Savior, Yeshua the Christ; to my dear husband, Garry; to our children: LaToya, Mechel, Cory, Andrea, Devin, Christopher, and Joshua; to our grandchildren: Zaria, Cameron, Ciara, and Cara; to my past; to my future; and it is dedicated to You.

To Michael & Katrina,
God Bless You
Sylvia G. Thomas
12/7/06

Always Trust in Jesus!

Acknowledgements

I wish to thank my loving mother, Noretta, who stood with me in the time of my greatest trials.

I also want to thank my brother, Ricky, and sister-in-law, Darlene, and their family for their constant love and support.

I want to thank my sister, Brenda, for always believing in her big sister.

I thank my Dad, Sylvester, and step mom, Sandy, for being there in my time of need.

I want to thank my sister, Cathy; my brother, Ronald; and my brother, Bryan; my sister-in-law, Jeannie, and their family for always supporting me.

I want to thank my mother-in-law, Eliza, for blessing our family in so many ways.

I want to thank my Aunt Etta and my grandmother-in-law, Mama Nina, for being wonderful examples for my life in love and marriage.

I want to thank my dear friends Venessa, Sylvia, Zenaida, John, and Pamela for their encouragement in my hour of need and their unwavering friendship during that time.

I want to thank Ms. Tramaine Hawkins who unknowingly ministered to me day in and day out through song.

My special thanks to my husband, Garry, for his love and patience and to all of my children who endured with me.

Introduction

One day I was walking around the park near my house. As I walked, I prayed, "Lord, please give me tough skin, please give me tough skin." I was in terrible anguish and I knew that I had to let God develop His weapons in me for me to battle the things I was going through.

It all started the day I gave my life to Jesus Christ. My transformation was especially difficult and the devil was not going to let this new life in Jesus Christ come easy for me. Neither my mind nor my flesh submitted willingly to the Lord bringing on severe demonic attacks upon my life. I had to learn how to use all of God's weapons that (Ephesians 6:1-18) talks about to fight. I also had to learn to speak God's Word against Satan's attacks. I learned to pray fervently without ceasing. I had to learn to cast every foul thought down in the name of Jesus.

Because of these demonic attacks, I had gone into deep depression and suffered a severe emotional breakdown. To add to my problems, I had divorced, after nine years, from a terribly abusive marriage. Now, as I walked, I was yet again having deep troubles in my second marriage. I spoke to the Lord, "What more can I go through?" What I didn't know was that everything was to get worse before it got better. Now, years later, I share with you the weapons and means to how I overcame depression and demonic oppression and how you can overcome those things with the Lord's help. It is my solemn prayer that this book will help and minister to all that are oppressed by the enemy, Satan.

I am happy to say that God did deliver me out of my troubles. Today, I am at peace with God, and I'm still with my husband fourteen years later and love him very much. I must add that God did indeed give me the "Tough Skin" that I asked for, and now Satan runs from me.

Sylvia A. Thomas

Sylvia A. Thomas

Chapter I

When the Going Gets Tough, the Tough Go to Jesus

I used to think that I was a tough person and could handle just about anything that came my way. In my family, I was considered the "strong" one. Then, my whole world came crushing down, and I was broken into a million little pieces until the Lord Jesus Christ came to my rescue and lifted me up and put my life back together again. It was then that I realized that it is ok to be tough—but only in Jesus Christ.

We have to have some backbone in this life to deal with the pressures that come our way, but we must be tough in Jesus Christ and Him alone. A car sticker that I used to have on my car expresses my sentiment:

"WHEN THE GOING GETS TOUGH, THE TOUGH GO TO JESUS."

A Tough World

You've got to be tough in this world to survive. I'm not talking about the toughness of the world with guns, knives, and fighting. I'm talking about being tough in Jesus; tough in prayer, tough in warfare, tough in standing against the wiles of the devil. Don't give up. You can't give up. You've got to keep on fighting the good fight of faith. *(1 Timothy 6:12).*

You've got to keep on until the end. Encourage yourself in the Lord with Scripture, song, and praise. Let the Lord lift you up out of the miry clay and the pit. *(Psalms 40:2).* Don't let anything get you down and keep you down.

Be watchful; be diligent, for Scripture says that your adversary, the devil, roams around like a roaring lion seeking whom he can devour. *(1 Peter 5:8).* But Scripture also says that Jesus came that we may have life and have it more abundantly. *(John 10:10).* We must go for and strive for strong faith in Jesus' promises. If He says that He came that we may have life more abundantly then look for it to happen. Expect it. Go for it in all that you do. Sure, the adversary is going to try to distract you, knock you down, and discourage you and even kill you. But keep your eyes on Jesus. If you become distracted for a short time, get your focus back. Look to your God and Savior who has richly endowed you with great promises throughout the Scripture if you are faithful and endure to the end. If you fall, get up. If you fall, get up. If you fall, get up. Keep trying.

One of the enemy's greatest weapons for keeping us down is depression. We wake up and don't want to face another day. We just want to pull the covers over our head and hope the day will pass us by without us being noticed. Start praying. Call out to Jesus who is Lord. Tell him how you feel; your innermost yearnings.

Get into His word. Read the Psalms. Read God's promises. Surround yourself with Christian literature and Christian music. We've got to fight the enemy with God's weapons. Get yourself up and confess who you are in Christ. You are a child of the King. He is the only God, the God of the universe, and He is able to deliver you from the feelings of depression and despair. Let God speak to your heart. He can help you to discern what is ailing you. Just be quiet for a while and listen to Him. We can't afford to wallow in self pity. It leads to nothing but further destruction. God calls His Saints to be strong in the faith; not those that give up with no hope. If you trust in Jesus, then there is always hope. Scripture tells us to always be ready to give an account for the hope that is in us when we are asked. *(1 Peter 3:15)*.

Jesus is hope. Even at your lowest point, when perhaps even contemplating suicide; STOP. Bring your thoughts back into captivity to the hope of glory, Jesus Christ. *(1 Corinthians 10:5)*.

Kneel before Him; reach out to Him. When words forsake you, moan and groan, for the Spirit of God even understands our groaning. *(Romans 8:26&27)*. God will lift you up if you let Him. Let Him.

Chapter II

Tough Skin

And having done everything to stand. Stand Firm. *(Ephesians 6:13&14)*

Imagine that your skin is tough—as tough as that of an alligator that nothing can pierce through. Imagine that you are like that of a ripe avocado with a rough textured outer exterior yet soft and smooth inside. These were the thoughts that came into my mind as I was writing this chapter. I thought—I need not to let anything pierce through my outer exterior that has the power to adversely control my thoughts, emotions and actions.

So stand tall with your head up, and be shielded.

Scripture tells us in Ephesians Chapter 6 to fight our daily battles with the weapons that God gives us. In this chapter—our weapon is the shield of faith in which we quench all of the fiery darts of the enemy.

Tough Skin

We need to pray for and develop tough skin. The enemy is constantly attacking us in our marriages, finances, and children or through illness. We must wake up alert everyday. We must be watchful and prayerful daily. *(Luke 21:36)*.

Satan is reminiscent of a gopher that digs holes all over the yard. When you go to a hole that the gopher has dug, he has already left that one and gone to another part of the yard and created another one. The devil goes from one area of our lives to another, creating holes in our lives. And we're standing around wondering what's happening, what's going on in our lives. He is trying to destroy us is what's happening. *(John 10:10)*.

He creates havoc in our finances which in turn puts great strain on our marriages, if married. He causes our children to misbehave which again causes a chain reaction in our marriages, if married, to try to destroy the marriage. If you're not married with children, these attacks still weigh heavily on the individual and can cause deep despair or depression. It gives us a feeling of helplessness, and we want to say the heck with trying anymore, I don't care what happens.

That is just where the enemy wants you and me, down and out with despair, hopelessness, and depression. We can't give in to him. We must pull out all the weapons of our warfare and fight. Scripture says, "The weapons of our warfare are not carnal but mighty in God for pulling down strongholds. *(2 Corinthians 10:4).*

So many people fail to realize that we are in a spiritual battle. When things happen to us one thing after the other, it is like Satan going from hole to hole, attacking us; throwing fiery darts. *(Ephesians 6:16).*

How do we fight all of these problems that come at us? Tough Skin. We need to see ourselves with thick textured skin, immovable and steadfast so that nothing the enemy throws our way can pierce through. Again Scripture tells us, "And having done everything to stand, stand firm". *(Ephesians 6:13&14).* We need to develop that stance. We need to grasp the full meaning of that statement. When the bills are overdue and the utility man comes to turn off the utilities, don't cry, don't shout, but stand, and see the toughness of your skin. Let nothing pierce through. Draw on your resources. Think. Ask God to show you a way. Remind Him of His promises to you.

God is faithful and just. How do we know? Because He says He is. Consider Psalm 36:5 which says, "Your Love, O Lord, reaches to the heavens, your faithfulness to the skies," and also Isaiah 45:21, "And there is no God apart from me, a righteous God and a Savior; there is none but me." Think back to areas God has delivered you and your family from. Think of what He has done for you. He is still the same God. He wants to deliver you from whatever you are facing right now. Have faith in Him.

Another great attack of the enemy is through other people. Satan constantly causes individuals to become angry or jealous of one another. However, we must remember that Scripture tells us that our fight is not against flesh and blood, or the carnal man; our fight is "against the powers of this dark world and against spiritual forces of evil in the heavenly realms." *Ephesians 6:10-20.*

The next time you have a disagreement with a loved one, or even an enemy, discern where the fight is coming from and who is causing it. Satan is often succeeding when he can cause continual conflict in our relationships. Scripture tells us to put on God's armor to fight our battles. Ephesians chapter 6:13-20 tells us exactly what that armor is. It lists six items of armor that God instructs us to wear to fight the enemy in this world. They are:

1. The Belt of Truth around your waist.

2. The Breastplate of Righteousness.

3. The Gospel of Peace on your feet.

4. The Shield of Faith to stop Satan's fiery darts.

5. The Helmet of Salvation.

6. The Sword of the Spirit which is the Word of God

God then tells us to pray on all occasions with all kinds of prayers and requests. His last command to us in this verse is to Be Alert. The command to wear God's armor to fight our earthly battles is our formula for successful spiritual warfare as well as physical battle on this earth.

Satan loves to deceive us into thinking that our meekness, gentleness, and quietness, the inner qualities that we get from God, are weaknesses. *(Galatians 5:22&23).* And we believe Satan. We do not have to let Satan run all over us while we are striving to live a meek and gentle life. God did not call us to be weak in the faith, neither male nor female. We all must strive to be strong mature Christians who can stand on our own two feet and at the same time have the fruit of meekness and gentleness. *(Ephesians 6:10)*.

Don't lose your fire, your motivation, or your persistence, as the Lord develops the fruit of the Spirit in you. We can not let the enemy lie to us that our meekness is weakness. Be strong in the Spirit of God. Don't let circumstances tear you down. Don't let people tear you down. Cast down pride, yet be strong in the Spirit of God.

God loves a perfect balance. *(Proverbs 11:1)*. Get balanced. Be meek, be gentle, be quiet, yet, be strong. Be tough in prayer. Develop tough skin.

Chapter III

Pray Without Ceasing

Pray Continually. *(1 Thessalonians 5:17)*

When I think about God, I think about praying. When I think about praying, I think about God and how He instructs us through His almighty Word to pray constantly. I think about the times my soul has been in such anguish that only God could remove my pain and help me see the light. I think about our Lord Jesus Christ and remember how He prayed unceasingly to our heavenly Father. I think about Gethsemane. I have learned first hand about the power of what it means to pray without ceasing. I have seen circumstances miraculously turned around through my own prayers. I have also seen the sick and the lame made well again through my laying hands on them and praying. I have even laid hands on myself and experienced the almighty power of God through Him making me well. Yes, there is Power in Prayer. It is our direct line to God through our Lord and Savior Jesus Christ and we must pray in order to live a victorious life while we transient through our journey on earth.

Prayer, Our Direct Line

The foundation of our Christian lives is prayer. Prayer is our direct communication to God. We must learn to pray and not only to pray but to pray without ceasing. *(1 Thessalonians 5:17) KJV.*

Pray when you rise in the morning. Pray throughout the day. Pray when circumstances arise. Pray when you need help at work. Pray when you're happy. Pray when you're sad. Pray at night before you retire. Pray with your husband. Pray with your wife. Pray with your children. Pray. If we want answers from God, we must pray. If we want mountains moved we must pray.

To have tough skin in a tough world, we must learn to pray what I call warfare praying. Warfare-praying consists of perseverance in prayer, persistence in prayer, lamenting, travailing, wailing, laying prostrate, groaning and speaking in tongues. We need to pray warfare-praying when we are in distress and need a breakthrough from God. We must empty ourselves out for God in order to receive the breakthrough we sometimes need. Ahead, I have outlined each of the components of warfare-praying:

Perseverance

"Consider it pure joy my brothers whenever you face trials of many kinds because you know that the testing of your faith develops perseverance. Perseverance must finish its work so that you may be mature and complete, not lacking anything." *(James 1:2-4).*

We must develop perseverance in prayer in our Christian journey. We must learn to stay constantly before the throne of God and not give up or think that He tires of hearing from us. He does not tire from hearing the cries of His people. God calls us to perseverance.

"Do you not know that in a race all the runners run, but only one gets the prize? Run in such a way as to get the prize." *(1 Corinthians 9:24).* Persevere in prayer.

Persistence

Then Jesus told his disciples a parable to show them that they should always pray and not give up. He said: "In a certain town there was a judge who neither feared God nor cared about men. And there was a widow in that town who kept coming to him with the plea, 'Grant me justice against my adversary.'"

For some time he refused. But finally he said to himself, "Even though I don't fear God or care about men, yet because this widow keeps bothering me, I will see that she gets justice, so that she won't eventually wear me out with her coming."

And the Lord said, "Listen to what the unjust judge says. And will not God bring justice for His chosen ones, who cry out to him day and night? Will He keep putting them off? I tell you, He will see that they get justice and quickly." *(Luke18 1-8).*

The widow in this parable was persistent. She would not give up which is likewise how we must be in our prayers. Surely, as the Scripture points out, God will bring justice to those that are His if we persist.

Luke 11:1-9 tells of how Jesus disciples asked Him to teach them how to pray. Jesus told them a parable of a man who had a friend that came to him in the middle of the night wanting to borrow three loaves for another friend who had come to him on his journey and he had no food to offer him. The first friend would not get up to give the second friend the loaves. The second friend was very persistent and because of his persistence, he obtained what he asked for. Jesus adds to the parable, "Ask and it will be given unto you, seek and you will find, knock and it will be opened to you." We must be persistent in prayer.

Lamenting, Travailing, and Wailing

"My God, my God, why have you forsaken me?

Why are you so far from saving me?"

So far from the words of my groaning.

O my God, I cry out by day but you do not answer,

by night, and am not silent."

(Psalms 22:1&2)

David cried out to God in the deepest anguish of his soul many times throughout the book of Psalms. We must do the same. Sometimes it takes getting before the Lord in sweat and tears for us to get a breakthrough from Him.

"Turn to me and be gracious to me,

for I am lonely and afflicted.

The troubles of my heart have multiplied;

free me from my anguish.

Look upon my affliction and my distress

and take away all my sins.

See how my enemies have increased

and how fiercely they hate me.

Guard my life and rescue me;

let me not be put to shame for I take refuge in you.

May integrity and uprightness protect me,

Sylvia A. Thomas

because my hope is in you."

(Psalms 25:16-21)

We must lament, travail, and wail in prayer when we are in despair.

Laying Prostrate

Meanwhile, Saul was still breathing out murderous threats against the Lord's disciples. He went to the high priest and asked him for letters to the synagogues in Damascus, so that if he found any there who belonged to the Way, whether men or women, he might take them as prisoners to Jerusalem. As he neared Damascus on his journey, suddenly a light from heaven flashed around him. He fell to the ground and heard a voice say to him, "Saul, Saul, why do you persecute me?"

Sometimes, this is just where the Lord wants us, on the ground prostrate before Him. *(Job 1:20).* We are in total surrender to God when we are in this position.

While Saul was slain in the Holy Spirit which is how he ended up on the ground, we can go to God and voluntarily lay before Him in our prayers as well as falling under the power of the Holy Spirit.

Groaning

"We know that the whole creation has been groaning as in the pain of childbirth right up to the present time. Not only so, but we ourselves, who have the first fruits of the Spirit, groan inwardly as we wait eagerly for our adoption as sons, the redemption of our bodies." *(Romans 8:22&23).*

We need not be hesitant to groan in our deepest prayers to God. The Holy Spirit can and does interpret our groans.

Praying in Other Tongues

"But you will receive power when the Holy Spirit comes upon you; and you will be my witnesses in all Jerusalem, and in all Judea and Samaria, and to the ends of the earth." *(Acts 1:8).* "All of them were filled with the Holy Spirit and began to speak in other tongues." *(Acts 2:4)*.

If you haven't been filled with the Holy Spirit and asked God for the gift of other tongues, you need to. This type of praying is imperative to walking a victorious Christian life and defeating Satan and his foes. When praying in other tongues, you will also defeat another great enemy; the flesh.

Sometimes we don't need to know what we are saying in prayer. When praying in other tongues, God knows what you are saying. Furthermore, praying in other tongues can help us to pray. In the same way, the Spirit helps us in our weakness. We do not know what we ought to pray for, but the Spirit Himself intercedes for us with groans that words cannot express. *(Romans 8:26)*.

We need to ask God for the gift of other tongues so that we may also be edified in prayer. "He who speaks in a tongue edifies himself." *(1 Corinthians 14:4)*. Warfare-praying is needed in the spiritual warfare that we experience in this day and time. If you are not warfare-praying, you need to be.

Chapter IV

The Word

When I was first introduced to the Word of God, The Holy Bible, I remember thinking about how magnificent it was that God, the Creator of the Universe and of mankind, gave us a handbook for our lives so that we would know Him and know how He wanted us to live and treat one another. That is exactly how I have used the Bible; as God's roadmap for my life. He tells us in Psalm 119:105, that His Word is a light for our path and a lamp for our feet. How truly awesome it is that God did not create us without giving us His divine direction and instruction for our journey back home.

The Awesome Word

Read the Word of God. Stand on the Word of God. Live by the Word of God. Be obedient to the Word of God. To have tough skin we must know who God is and what He promises us. His nature is revealed to us in His Word, the Holy Scriptures. We must get His Word in our Spirits so when troubles flood us; the Holy Spirit can fight through us by bringing appropriate Scripture to our remembrances. We must know how to fight in spiritual warfare based on what we know the Word of God to say.

The Holy Scriptures were written for our instruction for living and to teach us how to stand in the day of terror. They are filled with promises for the faithful and righteous. We need to be diligent about reading the Word of God daily. Set aside some time to spend in Scripture. Memorize it. Confess it with your mouth. Get it in your spirit. Invoke the Holy Spirit to help you.

I have compiled this collection of Psalms and Scriptures to help you in developing tough skin. Read them. Meditate on them. Rely on them for they are the written Word of God.

"I sought the Lord and He answered me;

He delivered me from all of my fears.

Those who look to Him are radiant;

their faces are never covered with shame."

(Psalm 34:4&5)

"Whoever of you loves life

and desires to see many good days,

keep your tongue from evil

and your lips from speaking lies."

(Psalm 34:12-14)

"Trust in the Lord and do good;

dwell in the land and enjoy safe pasture.

Delight yourself in the Lord

and He will give you the desires of your heart."

"Commit your way to the Lord;

trust in Him and He will do this:

He will make your righteousness shine like the dawn,

Sylvia A. Thomas

the justice of your cause like the noonday sun.

Be still before the Lord and wait patiently for Him."

(Psalm 37:3-7a)

"God is our refuge and strength,

an ever-present help in trouble."

(Psalm 46:1)

"Surely God is my help;

the Lord is the one who sustains me."

(Psalm 54:4)

"Guard my life, for I am devoted to you.

You are my God, save your servant

who trusts you.

Tough Skin

Have mercy on me, O Lord

for I call to you all day long."

(Psalm 86:2&3)

"In the day of my trouble I will call to you,

for you will answer me."

(Psalm 86:7)

"Yet the Lord longs to be gracious to you;

He rises to show you compassion.

For the Lord is a God of justice.

Blessed are all who wait for Him!"

(Isaiah 30:18)

"Those who hope in the Lord

will renew their strength.

they will soar on wings like eagles

they will run and not grow weary

Sylvia A. Thomas

they will walk and not faint."

(Isaiah 40:31)

"Therefore, since Christ suffered in His body,

arm yourselves also with the same attitude,

because He who has suffered in His body

is done with sin."
(1Peter 4:1)

"Finally, be strong in the Lord and His mighty power.

Put on the full armor of God so that you can stand

against the devil's schemes."

(Ephesians 6:10&11)

Chapter V

Obedience

To obey is better than sacrifice. *(1 Samuel 15:22)*

I can remember that as a babe in Christ, the thing I wanted most in life was to obey the Lord Jesus Christ. That was not always an easy task because although the preacher would often tell us to just listen to the voice of the Lord, how was I to know when I was really hearing His voice? Was I to listen to an audible voice or a spiritual inner voice? I have learned to listen to the Lord and have realized that He indeed speaks to His people in many different ways. He speaks audibly to His people, but more often, He speaks to us in a small inner voice that we must train ourselves to hear. He also speaks to us in His written Word, the Holy Bible, through other people, and through circumstances. We must learn to obey our Lord. We must learn to hear Him when He speaks. Jesus Himself tells us in the book of John 10:27 that His sheep hear His voice. I have found that I hear the voice of the Lord most often in the quiet. Take some time regularly to "Just Be Quiet."

The Obedient Heart

God wants our obedience. We must obey the commands of the Word of God to have tough skin in this life. If God says do not lie, then do not lie. If He says do not steal, then do not steal. *(Leviticus 19:11).*

We must strive to be perfect in Christ. We are not perfect but we can strive to be. Strive for excellence. We do not have a leg to stand on if we are not in God's obedience. How can we expect God to work for our behalf in our finances, for example, if we are not giving back from the increase that He gives us. We must be obedient for God to be able to bless us financially. Otherwise, we suffer the consequences. To be tough in a tough world, we must be able to stand on our obedience to God. Then we can go to God and say, "Lord, I have been faithful in this thing and I am trusting in your promise to me for my obedience." The promise of what, you may ask? The promise of keeping us healthy, keeping us safe from danger, keeping our minds sound, keeping our marriages together or prosperity. Whatever you are believing God for, it takes obedience to Him in order to receive it. In Deuteronomy, Scripture tells us this concerning obedience:

"If you fully obey the Lord your God and carefully follow all His commands I give you today, the Lord your God will set you high above all nations on earth.

All these blessings will come upon you and accompany you if you obey the Lord your God:

You will be blessed in the city and blessed in the country.

The fruit of your womb will be blessed, and the crops of your land and the young of your livestock, the calves of your herds and the lambs of your flocks.

Your basket and your kneading through will be blessed.

You will be blessed when you come in and blessed when you go out.

The Lord will grant that the enemies who rise up against you will be defeated before you. They will come at you from one direction but flee from you seven.

The Lord will send a blessing on your barns and on everything you put your hand to. The Lord your God will bless you in the land He is giving you.

The Lord will establish you as His holy people, as He promised you on oath, if you keep the commands of the Lord your God and walk in His ways.

Then all the peoples on earth will see that you are called by the name of the Lord, and they will fear you.

The Lord will grant you abundant prosperity, in the fruit of your womb, the young of your livestock and the crops of your ground, in the land He swore to your forefathers to give.

The Lord will open the heavens, the storehouse of His bounty, to send rain on your land in season and to bless all the work of your hands. You will lend to many nations but will borrow from none.

The Lord will make you the head, not the tail. If you pay attention to the commands of the Lord your God that I give you this day and carefully follow them, you will always be at the top, never at the bottom. Do not turn aside from any of the commands I give you today, to the right or to the left, following other gods and serving them." *(Deuteronomy 28:1-14)*

Sometimes we are just not sure what God is saying to us. If in doubt, line it up with Scripture. Do what Scripture commands. Make sure that what you are hearing or have been told is in obedience to what Scripture says. Listen to the Lord. Find quiet time out of each day, even if only for ten minutes, to be still and hear from God. He often speaks to our hearts in the quiet. *(1 Kings 19:11&12)*.

Sylvia A. Thomas

When we know what God is saying to us and are obedient, then, we can walk upright. We can be immovable and not allow the storms of life to blow us over. We will not be tossed to and fro with every wind of doctrine, but will be standing on the Word of God and our obedience to it. *(Ephesians 4:14)*.

If we do not learn to obey God, stand and have tough skin in battle all of the time, then Satan can rob us. The thief comes to steal, kill, and destroy. *(John 10:10)*.

We must always be aware of that. We can not let our guards down. In our obedience to reading the Word of God, we are equipped for every good work. *(2 Timothy 2:14-20)*. Furthermore, we are also equipped to fight the good fight of faith. *(2 Timothy 4:7)*.

Learn obedience to God. Find out what God is saying to you specifically in all that you do. Seek after Him with your whole heart and He will reveal Himself to you. As you obey Him, He will do as He promises and guard the faithful. *(Psalm 97:10)*.

He will be there for you in the face of death, illness and destruction. And you will be able to stand against the schemes of Satan because you are tough through obedience.

Chapter VI

The Embattled Mind

Day after day

there is the fight

of internal conflict

I love with all my heart

and all my voice

but, the mind is a battlefield

And now Lord, what do I wait for?

My hope is in thee

Satan had me where he wanted me for a short time in my life

because he was clever in attacking me where I was most

vulnerable—in my mind. He almost succeeded in killing me as I

suffered from extreme depression and low self esteem.

The attack from Satan for my mind and body was a fierce

one. However, I fought it to the bitter end until I got the complete victory in my Lord Jesus who I always knew was greater and more powerful than this enemy that was trying to destroy me. I held on to the Lord Jesus and His Word with all of my might to gain my victory. I pulled out all of the weapons of my warfare that God had promised me in His Written Word so that I could fight this ferocious enemy. Not in my strength but only in Christ did I gain my victory. Don't stand by and let Satan succeed in what he is here for which is to steal, kill, and destroy. Fight with all your might and Jesus will already be way ahead of you. "The victory is yours in Christ."

The Devil's Playing Field

In order to develop tough skin, we now need to talk about what goes on in the mind. The mind is Satan's battlefield where he attacks and controls us. The mind is filled with internal conflict. We must become renewed in our minds if we are going to win this earthly battle. We must change our thinking. Scripture says, "Do not conform any longer to the pattern of this world, but be transformed by the renewing of your mind." *(Romans 12:2).*

Satan attacks the mind and fills it with evil thoughts by using such things as the books we read, the music we listen to, and the art that we look at. Evil surrounds us. We need to stop reading material for enjoyment that involves the occult or murderous mysteries, if we want to live a victorious Christian life. We need to pay close attention to the lyrics we listen to in song. We need to notice the deeper meaning of much of the art that we look at or have in our homes and businesses. There are subliminal messages. Our children are being filled with them everyday at such places as innocent as school. Pay attention to the books your child brings home from their school library. Many of them are filled with the occult. "Let those who love the Lord hate evil, for He guards the lives of His faithful ones and delivers them from the hand of the wicked." *(Psalm 97:10).*

We let God renew our minds in several different ways. First of all, it is through Scripture. Learning what the Word of God says about all things is the beginning of mind renewal. As we learn what it says, we need to memorize it, confess it and live it. "Be doers of the Word and not hearers only." *(James 1:22).*

As you do this, God will show you His ways and what to think about and look at. He will cleanse your thoughts and fill them with the things of God. You will begin to notice and appreciate God in the beauty of creation. You will no longer desire the horrendous things of an un-renewed mind in the books you read and the music you listen to.

"Finally, brothers, whatever is true, whatever is noble, whatever is right, whatever is pure, whatever is lovely, whatever is admirable—if anything is excellent or praiseworthy—think about such things." *(Philippians 4:8).*

Once the mind is renewed in a certain area, we must battle Satan to keep our minds clear. We do battle by casting down thoughts and imaginations that exalt themselves against God. *(2 Corinthians 10:5).*

You may ask, how does one cast down thoughts? By rebuking them, that is how. You can say in your mind or verbally, "I rebuke that thought in the name of Jesus, I cast it down." A new

Christian may find themselves repeating this all day long until they get stronger in their minds. Eventually, you will have victory over Satan and the evil thoughts he sends your way. Be encouraged.

You may find it helpful to find certain Scriptures to stand on when having battle in the mind. Once you find them, write them down and read and confess them daily until you have victory in your thoughts. We should be able to put every thought into captivity to Jesus Christ. *(2 Corinthians 10:5).*

Another culprit to the mind is clutter. The mind can become over burdened and cluttered with such things as worry and un-forgiveness. Scripture says, "Therefore do not worry about tomorrow, for tomorrow will worry about itself. Each day has enough trouble of its own." *(Matthew 6:34).* God knows your need even before you ask and He will come through for you if you truly learn to trust Him.

Unforgiveness, the other big mind clutterer, puts a block between God and us. We must not let the bad thoughts we harbor towards someone take over our thoughts. If you are harboring un-forgiveness, you need to deal with it. Unforgiveness should be dealt with immediately. If you are having a problem with someone, try this: Write them a long letter telling them what is on your mind, and do not mail it. Doing this will help you come to terms with the issues that are upsetting you, and you will be able to forgive the person. Other ways of getting rid of unforgiveness are prayer, going to the individual and talking it out or seeking professional counseling. How ever you decide to deal with it is up to you. Do not let unforgiveness be your block to God.

In conclusion, we need to think about what we are thinking about. We must not let everything that comes in our mind stay there because a lot of it does not belong there. Let God cleanse your thoughts and give you a new way of thinking.

Chapter VII

Love Yourself

I had to learn to love "Me." I had to learn to embrace who I was as a little girl as well as whom I had become as a grown woman. If we do not love ourselves, it is virtually impossible to love others. In order for us to love ourselves, we must first learn to forgive ourselves. Remember that Jesus paid the ultimate price for mankind so that we would be forgiven by God for all of our wrongdoings. If God can and has forgiven us than, we negate that fact by not forgiving ourselves. We are essentially putting ourselves higher than our Lord in our lives when we do not forgive ourselves. After years of not loving myself and suffering from a counter-productive low self esteem, I now know the true depth of God's love for me and can honestly say, I Love Sylvia.

You Are Important

Loving yourself is imperative to having tough skin. We cannot stand in these perilous times if we have no love for ourselves or do not take care of ourselves. Just as it takes a great amount of training for athletic activities, likewise, we must train diligently for the Christian life. Such training takes time, dedication, energy, continued practice, and diligence. We are not up for this task if we fail to care for ourselves.

"Do you not know that in a race all the runners run, but only one gets the prize? Run in such a way as to get the prize. Everyone who competes in the games goes into strict training. They do it to get a crown that will not last; but we do it to get a crown that will last forever. Therefore, I do not run like a man running aimlessly; I do not fight like a man beating the air." *(1 Corinthians 9:24-26).*

In order to run this race, we must be physically fit. Get some exercise each week. Take your multiple vitamin daily as well as other vitamin and mineral supplements. Do not abuse your body with drugs, alcohol, and cigarettes. Show God that you are

Sylvia A. Thomas

interested in your health and that you are investing in it. Show Him that you care about you. Our bodies are the temple of God. He lives in us so take care of your body. *(1 Corinthians 3:16).*

Take time out for yourself as well. We all need to be able to have solitude in our spirits sometimes. Spend time in prayer. Spend time in meditation. Sit in God's presence in silence for a while and enjoy the peace of God. Our days are filled with so much activity. We need to settle ourselves down daily and go to a quiet place. Jesus says in Mark 6:31, "Come with me by yourselves to a quiet place and get some rest."

Get yourself a hobby. Find something you enjoy doing and learn to do it well. Learn a sport; read a good book. You are not too young or to old. You are just right to learn to take time out and care for yourself.

Women, take care of your skin. Use facial cleanser, astringent, and moisturizer. Fix your hair. Adorn yourself. Let your clothing be holiness, righteousness, gentleness, and peace. Be beautiful inside and out.

Men, as well, take care of your skin. Give yourself a nice shave. Get a haircut. Clothe yourself in the righteousness and strength of God. Look your best. Be your best.

We need to learn to be positive. We have to stop thinking and acting negatively. Learn to give yourself positive self talk. For example, *I Can Do It; I Will Succeed; I Am Kind; or Jesus Loves Me.* Tell yourself good things. Make positive statements and be optimistic.

"Love believes all things." *(1 Corinthians 13:6).* A negative attitude actually reflects a lack of faith and "without faith it is impossible to please God." *(Hebrews 11:6).* Have faith in God. Believe Him.

Be tough in mind, body, and spirit. "Fight the good fight of faith, finish the race and keep the faith." *(2 Timothy 4:7).*

Chapter VIII

Choose Life

God is a God of choices. He did not create people as robots but instead gave us a will and conscience so that we can make choices for ourselves. When I am faced with choices, I generally will weigh the consequences and try to make a well thought out godly choice for myself. People can choose to follow God or not to follow God. When we choose not to follow God, we have automatically by default chosen to follow the enemy of God, the devil. I am personally so happy and blessed that I made the choice when the Lord gave it to me, to follow Him. It was the best and most important life decision that I have ever made. However, that was only the beginning of the constant daily decisions to follow Jesus and it has not always been easy. Sometimes I have made mistakes and made the wrong choice and many times I have had to suffer hurting consequences. But, I always give myself credit that at least I try to make the right

choice and with that, I have the confidence that Jesus will always

correct my ways and show me the right choice. Make your

choice.

Choose Life; Choose Jesus!

Life is Good

"See, I set before you today life and prosperity, death and

destruction. For I command you today to love the Lord

your God, to walk in His ways, and to keep His commands,

decrees and laws; then you will live and increase, and the

Lord your God will bless you in the land you are entering

to possess. But if your heart turns away and you are not

obedient, and if you are drawn away to bow down to other

gods and worship them, I declare to you this day that you

will certainly be destroyed. You will not live long in the

land you are crossing the Jordan to enter and possess.

This day I call heaven and earth as witnesses against you

that I have set before you life and death, blessings and

curses. Now choose life, so that you and your children may

live and that you may love the Lord your God, listen to His

voice, and hold fast to Him. For the Lord is your life, and

He will give you many years in the land He swore to give to

your fathers, Abraham, Isaac, and Jacob."

(Deuteronomy 30:15-20)

It is evident, according to Scripture, that we make our choices in life. We choose to be happy or sad, blessed or cursed. We can become depressed merely by what we think about and our physiology. If we think negative thoughts and hold our head down and slump our shoulders over, then we are sure to become depressed. It is hard to be anything else in that position. Therefore, we have made the choice to be depressed. On the other hand, if we tell ourselves positive things and hold our heads up, we have created a much more ecstatic attitude and physiology.

We choose life by what we eat as well. If we eat healthy, water-rich foods, we have chosen life. If we exercise regularly, we have chosen life. Again, the flip side of this is that if you do the adverse; eating fatty, unhealthy foods, overeating and never exercising, you have chosen death or a curse. In addition to that, if you are destroying your temple with drugs, alcohol and other debilitating products, then, again, you have chosen death versus life.

The pinnacle of all of these things is to follow Jesus Christ the Lord. When you are faithful in your journey with Jesus, you have chosen life. He will help you to be happy, eat healthy, exercise more, and put away alcohol, drugs and cigarettes, if you ask Him to.

The choice to receive blessing or cursing, life or death, is yours. Obey God, choose life and trust in Jesus so that you can withstand the perils of this life with *Tough Skin.*

Prayer for Salvation

If you do not know the Lord Jesus Christ as your personal Savior and would like to, then please pray this prayer for the cleansing of your sins and eternal salvation.

Dear Heavenly Father,

I come before you asking for the gift of your Dear Son Jesus to enter into my life and save me from eternal damnation. I am a sinner and pray for you to cleanse my heart from sin. I ask for your forgiveness. I ask Jesus to be my Lord from this day forward and to guide me. I humbly thank you, dear Lord, for saving me and giving me eternal life by sacrificing your own life and dying on a cross for me. Please help me to walk in my new life. In Jesus' name I pray, Amen.

Praise the Lord! The angles in heaven are rejoicing that you are now saved to eternal life and Jesus Christ is your Lord!

Tell somebody, get yourself a Holy Bible and get to know your Lord and Savior Jesus Christ.

References

1. All Scripture quoted from the New International Version of the Holy Bible unless otherwise noted.

2. Anthony Robbins; A Black Choice by Anthony Robbins

3. Poem "The Embattled Mind" written and copyrighted © by Sylvia A. Thomas 1996.

Reverend Sylvia A. Thomas

Sylvia A.   Thomas is also the author of *"Me? Jewish? The Revelation of a Black American Christian Jewish Woman."*

Sylvia A. Thomas books can be ordered online at:

www.amazon.com
www.barnesandnoble.com
www.booksamillion.com

Sylvia can be contacted at:

Sylvia Thomas Ministries
P. O. Box 13643
Tallahassee, FL 32317
www.NewIsraelOnline.org
SylviaThomasMinistries@yahoo.com

<u>Notes</u>

Printed in the United States
57187LVS00007B/451-552